WHY THE hell AM I IN debt?

Advantage
INSPIRATIONAL

A. RONALD COADY

Why The Hell Am I in Debt? by A. Ronald Coady
© 2005 by A. Ronald Coady
All Rights Reserved.
ISBN: 1-59755-040-X

Published by: ADVANTAGE BOOKS™
<u>www.advbooks.com</u>

This book and parts thereof may not be reproduced in any form, stored in a retrieval system or transmitted in any form by any means (electronic, mechanical, photocopy, recording or otherwise) without prior written permission of the author, except as provided by United States of America copyright law.

Unless otherwise indicated, Bible quotations are taken from the King James Version of the Bible

Bible quotation taken from *THE MESSAGE.* Copyright 1993, 1994, 1995 Eugene H. Peterson. Used by permission of Nav Press Publishing Group.

Library of Congress Control Number: 2005932972

First Printing: September 2005
09 10 11 12 01 02 03   9 8 7 6 5 4 3 2 1
Printed in the United States of America

Why the Hell Am I in Debt?

Dedication

This book is lovingly dedicated to the fond memories of my beloved wife, Muriel Coady and my dearest daughter, Joy Vickery whose constant encouragement and invaluable suggestions have made this work possible. They are sadly missed.

Memory Eternal O Lord

A. Ronald Coady

Disclaimer

The recommendations suggested in this book are neither professional nor legal advice. The reader is cautioned that before adopting these recommendations, he or she should seek counseling from reputable financial advisors or attorneys who specialize in the areas recommended.

The writer does not assume responsibility for any adverse outcome experienced by the reader in adopting his recommendations.

The Author

A. Ronald Coady

Acknowledgements

The author wishes to acknowledge the following persons and their works.

Evangelist John Avanzini, who is know in Christian circles as, 'The Apostle of Finance.' His lectures and books have been an inspiration and blessing to me.

Napoleon Hill's epic book, *Think and Grow Rich*. It has inspired and blessed me since first reading it in 1961.

Then, there is the small book, *The Richest Man in Babylon*, by George S. Clason. This work tied many loose ends together for me.

I have adapted some of the suggestions in these works in, *Why the Hell Am I in Debt?*

My dear friend, David Westbrook, who resides with his wife, Jocelyn in Sydney, Australia, did the art illustrations in this book.

A. Ronald Coady

David came to a saving knowledge of Jesus Christ during my Divine Healing Crusades in the Nelson/Richmond area in New Zealand in the early 1960's.

While attending my Bible School in Nelson, he did art work for me illustrating, 'The Tabernacle of Moses' and the, 'Book of Revelation.'

We renewed our friendship when I was visiting Australia two years ago. I told him of this book and asked him if he would do the illustrations for it. He graciously accepted. He has done an outstanding job. Thank you, David. Muriel and Joy would be proud.

Table of Contents

Prologue 11

Forward 15

The Seven Building Blocks for Building Your Own Personal Fortune

Chapter One 19
First Building Block
Start Your Exhausted Wallet to Overflowing

Chapter Two 29
Second Building Block
How to Master Your Expenses I

Chapter Three 33
How to Master Your Expenses II
Debt Destruction – Strategy for Debt Destruction

Chapter Four 43
Third Building Block
Start Multiplying Your Savings

Chapter Five 49
Fourth Building Block
Guard Your Savings

Chapter Six 51
Fifth Building Block
Protecting Your Family's Inheritance

Chapter Seven 63
Sixth Building Block
Insuring a Future Income

Chapter Eight 67
Seventh Building Block
Increasing Your ability to Learn and Earn

Appendix I 73
Miracle Debt Cancellation

Appendix II 79
The Lord's Portion – Tithes and Offerings

Appendix III 91
Wisdom Defined

Appendix IV 93
Securing for Yourself Gainful Employment

Epilogue 99

About The Author 101

Prologue

Positioning Yourself for Success

"Most people would succeed in small things if they were not troubled with great ambitions."
Henry Wadsworth Longfellow

It is an incontrovertible fact that God's desire for his people is for them to be successful in life right here on planet Earth.

In the third epistle of John, verse two, we read: ***"Beloved, I wish above all things that thou mayest prosper and be in health even as thy soul prospers."***

In the book of Joshua, chapter one and verse eight, God says to Joshua: ***"This book of the law shall not depart out of thy mouth; but thou shalt meditate therein day and night, that thou mayest observe to do according to all that is written therein: for then thou shalt make thy way prosperous, and then thou shalt have good success."***

Success means different things to different people. What does being successful in life mean to you?

The following are some definitions that any standard Dictionary will give you for the word 'success:'

Attainment, achievement, prosperity, flourishing, thriving, affluent, rich, wealthy, well off.

All of these are true, yet something seems to be missing. What about **FULLFILLMENT?**

You may achieve all of the above and yet remain unfulfilled.

Success Or Ambition – Which?

Before proceeding further we need to know the difference between **'success motivation'** and **"ambition." Ambition is an inordinate desire to attain wealth, power, and fame at any cost. It will trample under foot, crush and/or destroy anyone who stands in the way of the attainment of its goal.**

On the other hand, I define *"Success"* as follows:

1. Success is the ability **to be** in life what you really want to be.

2. Success is the ability to get out of life all that you desire without violating the rights of others.

No one succeeds alone. A successful person will take others with him up the Ladder of Success.

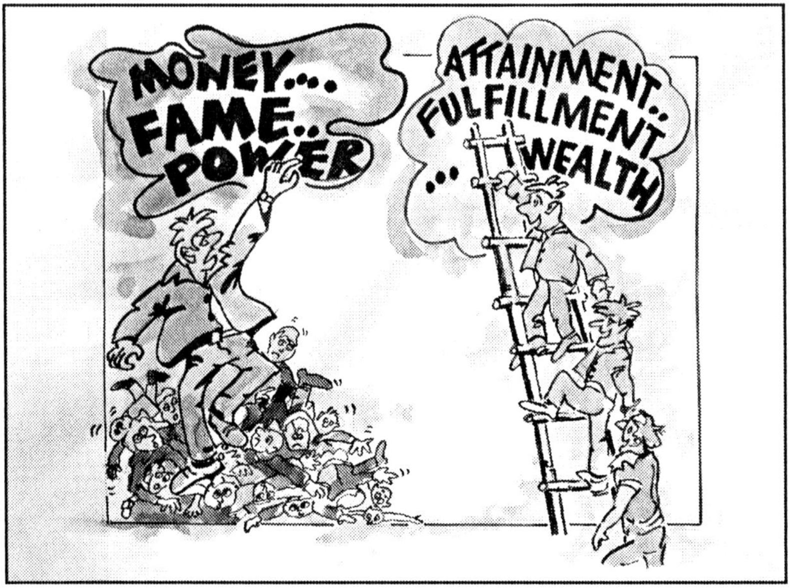
MONEY....
FAME..
POWER
ATTAINMENT..
FULFILLMENT
... WEALTH

Foreword

Solomon, in the book of Ecclesiastes writes, ***"Moreover the profit of the earth is for all."*** **Ecc. 5:9** Yet it is evident that the vast majority of the people of God are not enjoying their fair share of the profits of the earth.

This book is written for the sole purpose of showing you how you may enjoy your portion of the earth's profits.

In the book of Deuteronomy, chapter 8, verse 18 we are told by God, ***"But thou shalt remember the LORD thy God: for it is he that giveth thee power to get wealth, that he may establish his covenant which he sware to thy fathers."***

Again, we read in Deuteronomy 11:18-21, ***"Therefore shall ye lay up these my words in your heart and soul,…That your days may be multiplied, and the days of your children…as days of heaven upon earth."***

Settle it in your heart now, once and for all, that the will of God for you is to:

(i)   Prosper and be in health
(ii)   Receive your portion of the earth's profits
(iii)   Have good success and
(iv)   Enjoy days of heaven on earth.

Let us know proceed to see how all of these things may be accomplished and enjoyed.

The Seven Basic Building Blocks For Building Your Personal Fortune

A. Ronald Coady

The First Building Block
Causing Your Billfold to Swell

Bible Readings: (Please ensure you read the following Scriptures before proceeding.)

Romans 10:17: ***It is written, Faith cometh by hearing, and hearing by the word of God."***

Matthew 25:14-29: *"The kingdom of heaven us as a man traveling into a far country, who called his own servants, and delivered unto them his goods. And unto one he gave five talents, to another two, and to another one; to every man according to his several ability; and straitway he took his journey.*

Then he that had received the five talents went and traded with the same and made them other five talents. And likewise he that had received the two, he also gained other two.

But he that had received one went and digged in the earth, and his lord's money.

After a long time the lord of those servants cometh, and reckoneth with them and so he that had received the five talents came and brought other five talents, saying, Lord, thou deliveredst to me five talents: behold, I have gained beside them five talents more.

His lord said unto him, Well done thou good and faithful servant: thou hast been faithful over a few things, I will make thee ruler over many things: enter thou into the joy of the lord.

He also that had received two talents came and said, Lord thou deliveredst unto me two talents: behold I have gained two other talents beside them.

Chapter One: Causing Your Billfold to Swell

His lord said unto him, Well done, good and faithful servant: thou has been faithful over a few things, I will make thee ruler over many things: enter thou into the joy of thy lord.

Then he which had received the one talent came and said, Lord, I knee thee that thou art an hard man, sowing where thou hast now sown and gathering where thou has not strawed: And I was afraid, and went and hid thy talent in the earth: Lo, there thou hast that is thine.

His lord answered and said unto him, Thou wicked and slothful servant, thou knewest that I reap where I sowed not, and gather where I have not strawed: Thou oughtest therefore to have put my money to the exchangers, and then at my coming I should have received my own with usury. Take therefore the talent from him, and give it unto him, which hath ten talents.

For unto everyone that hath shall be given more, and he shall have abundance: But from him that hath not shall be taken away even that which he hath."

Psalm 112:1-3 & 5: *"Praise ye the LORD. Blessed is the man that feareth the LORD, that delighteth greatly in the LORD and that delightest greatly in his commandments.*

His seed shall be mighty upon the earth: the generation of the upright shall be blessed. Wealth and riches are in his house: and his righteousness endureth for ever. A good man sheweth favour, and lendeth: he will guide his affairs with discretion."

Proverbs 6:6-9: *"Go to the ant thou sluggard; consider her ways and be wise. Which having no guide, or overseer, or ruler, provideth her meat in the summer, and gathereth her food in the harvest."*

Proverbs 30:25-25: *"There be four things which are little upon the earth, but they are exceeding wise: The ants are a people not strong, yet they prepare their meat in the summer."*

Genesis 8:22: *"While the earth remaineth, seed time and harvest, cold and heat, summer and winter, and day and night shall not cease."*

There are many ways in which a person may earn dollars and cents. Each of these ways is a **'stream of wealth'**, which the laborer diverts, by his labor, a portion into his or her billfold. Into each of our billfolds there flows a stream of dollars and cents, large or small, according to each one's ability to earn a livelihood.

If you desire to build a personal fortune, you must begin by utilizing that source of money which you have already established.

Chapter One: Causing Your Billfold to Swell

For every $10 you put in your billfold, **LEAVE ONE DOLLAR IN IT.** What will happen? In time **YOUR BILLFOLD WILL EXPAND AND OVERFLOW.** Why? Because soon there will be **more** in your billfold than you are taking out!

This is the first building block to lay in order to build your personal fortune. It is the first element to commence your emaciated billfold to fattening and swelling. For every $10 you put in your billfold, take out nine for use and **leave one in.** Your billfold will begin to expand and fatten immediately. The increased amount will feel good in your hand and will bring delight to your soul.

Here is a strange reality. When you cease to pay out more than eight tenths of your earnings, you will manager to get along just as well as you did before. You will discover that your money is not shorter than before.

You will also discover that, ---it appears to be a God-ordained principle---those who keep back and spend not a certain amount of their earnings, wealth comes more readily. It is also a strange anomaly that wealth and good fortune seem to avoid the person whose billfold is empty!

Joseph in Egypt is an excellent example of these facts. Let us turn to the Word of God.

Genesis 41: 28-42 & verse 57: ***What God is about to do he sheweth unto Pharaoh. Behold, there come seven years of great plenty throughout all the land of Egypt. And there shall arise after them seven years of famine; and all the plenty shall be forgotten in the land of Egypt and the famine shall consume the land. And the plenty shall not be known in the land by reason of that famine following; for it shall be very grievous. And for that the dream was doubled unto Pharaoh twice; It is because the thing is established by God, and God will shortly bring it to pass.***

Now therefore let Pharaoh look out a man discreet and wise and set him over the land of Egypt in the seven plenteous years. Let Pharaoh do this, and let him appoint officers over the land, and take up the fifth part of the land of Egypt in the seven plenteous years. And let them gather all the food of those good years that come, and lay up corn under the hand of Pharaoh, and let them keep food in the cities. And that food shall be for store to the land against the seven years of famine, which shall be in the land of Egypt; that the land perish not.

And the thing was good in the eyes of Pharaoh and the eyes of all his servants. And Pharaoh said unto his servants, Can we find such an one as this is, a man in whom the Spirit of God is? And Pharaoh said unto Joseph, Forasmuch as God hath shewed thee all this, there is none so discreet and wise as thou art:

Thou shalt be over my house, and according to thy word shall all my people be ruled: only in the throne will I be greater than thou. And Pharaoh said unto Joseph, See, I have set thee over all the land of Egypt. And Pharaoh took off his ring from his hand and put it upon Joseph's hand, and arrayed him in vestures of fine linen and put a gold chain about his neck."

Genesis 41:47-49 & 53-57: *"And in the seven plenteous years the earth brought forth by the handfuls. And he gathered up all the food of the seven years, which were in the land of Egypt, and he laid up the food in the cities: the food of the field, which was round about every city, laid he up in the same.*

And the seven years of plenteousness, that was in the land of Egypt, were ended. And the seven years of dearth began to come according as Joseph had said: and the dearth was in all lands; but in all the land of Egypt there was bread.

And when all the land of Egypt was famished, the people cried to Pharaoh for bread: and Pharaoh said unto all the Egyptians, Go to Joseph; what he saith to you, do.

And the famine was over all the face of the earth: and Joseph opened all the storehouses, and sold unto the Egyptians; and the famine waxed sore in the land of Egypt.

And all countries came into Egypt to Joseph for to buy corn; because that the famine was so sore in all lands."

What do you desire more? Is it the gratification of passing desires – jewelry, a piece of finery, designer clothing, gourmet food, etc.? Such things are here today and gone tomorrow. They are quickly forgotten.

Or is your desire for **'substantial holdings,'** such as money, a home, property, a future income, sound investments, etc.?

The money you **take** from your billfold will bring the first. The money you **leave** in your billfold will bring the second!

The first basic building block to lay down for building your personal fortune is capsulated in the following motto, which is to be your adopted rule of conduct:

"For each $10 I put in my billfold I will spend only nine."

Remember the following maxim and remember it well:

"A part of all you earn is yours to keep."

Personalize it. Make it your daily confession – knowing that Jesus is the High Priest of your

Chapter One: Causing Your Billfold to Swell

confession, Heb. 3:1. Affirm it in a loud voice over and over: <u>A part of all I earn is mine to keep.</u>

A. Ronald Coady

Chapter Two

The Second Building Block
Mastering Your Expenses
Part I

Do you control your expenses or do they control you?

The majority of wage earners find that what they earn is not enough for their necessary expenses. How then can we keep one tenth for ourselves?

Here is another unusual truth: what we call, **'necessary expenses'** will always grow to equal our income unless we protest to the contrary.

Don't confuse 'necessary expenses' with DESIRES.

In Ecclesiastes 6:9, we read, *"Better is the sight of the eyes than the wandering of desire: this also is vanity and vexation of spirit."*

Each one of us, together with our family, has more desires than our earnings can gratify. Our earnings are spent as far s they can go to satisfy these desires. Yet, there remain many desires that are ungratified! All of us are burdened with more desires than we can gratify. How do you deal with this enigma? You must first realize that there are limits to:

(i) **Your time**
(ii) **Your strength**
(iii) **The distance you may travel**
(iv) **What you eat and drink**
(v) **The enthusiasm with which you may enjoy life.**

Examine carefully the accustomed habits of your lifestyle in these areas; in these areas certain expenses will be found that can be eliminated.

Your aim should be: **<u>One hundred percent of appreciated value demanded for every penny spent.</u>**

Be diligent in applying this principle. We are instructed in the book of Proverbs, ***"He becometh poor that dealeth with a slack hand: but the hand of the diligent maketh rich. He that gathereth in summer is a wise son: but he that sleepeth in harvest is a son that causeth shame."*** Prov. 10:4-5.

You may ask, "How do I start?"

(a) Select those desires that are necessary and others that are possible through the

expenditure of the eight tenths of your earnings.

(b) Eliminate the rest and consider them as a part of that great multitude of ungratified desires and sorrow not over them.

Next, **budget your necessary expenses.** Your first debtor is the Lord. **Touch not the Lord's Tithes (nor the one tenth kept in your billfold.)** You now have eight tenths to work with.

Keep working on your budget. Keep adjusting it. In doing this you will make it your **First Assistant** in causing your 'emaciated wallet to bulge.'

Now give attention to the Word of the Lord: *"Ye have sown much, and bring in little: ye eat, but ye have not enough; ye drink, but ye are not filled with drink; ye clothe you, but there is none warm; and he that earneth wages earneth wages to put it into a bag with holes. Thus said the LORD of hosts; Consider your says."*
"You looked for much, and, lo, it came to little; and when ye brought it home, I did blow upon it. Why? Saith the LORD of hosts. Because of mine house that is waste, and ye run every man unto his own house." Haggai 1:6-7 & 9

Again, hear the Voice of the Lord saying: *"Will a man rob God? Yet have ye robbed me. But ye say, Wherein have we robbed thee? In tithes and offerings. Ye are cursed with a curse: for ye have robbed me, even this whole nation.*

Bring ye all the tithes into the storehouse, that there may be meat in mien house, and prove me now herewith, saith the LORD of hosts, if I will not open you the windows of heaven and pour you out a blessing, that there shall not be room enough to receive it.

And I will rebuke the devourer for your sakes, and he shall not destroy the fruits of your ground: neither shall your vine cast her fruit before the time in the field, saith the LORD of hosts. And all nations shall call you blessed: for you shall be a delightsome land, saith the LORD of hosts." Malachi 3:8-12.

(For further teaching on Tithing, see Appendix II, **"The Lord's Portion – Tithes & Offerings."**)

Chapter Three

Mastering Your Expenses
Part II
Debt Destruction
Strategy and Tactic

Solomon writes in the book of Ecclesiastes, chapter seven, and verse 12: *"For wisdom is a defense, and money is a defense: but the excellency of knowledge is, that wisdom giveth life to them that have it."*

Again he writes, in chapter 10 verse 19: *"A feast is made for laughter, and wine maketh merry: but money answereth all things."*

The Apostle James writes in his epistle, chapter 1, verses 5-7: *"If any of you lack wisdom, let him ask of God, that giveth to all men liberally, and upbraideth not; and it shall be given him. But let him ask in faith, nothing wavering. For he that wavereth is like a wave of the sea driven with the wind and tossed. For let not that man think that he shall receive any thing of the Lord. A double minded man is unstable in all his ways."*

Wisdom is the ability or skill in taking what you know and using it to advantage in blessing others and yourself. In order words it is **now how!** (For a more complete definition of 'wisdom,' see Appendix III **"What is Wisdom?**)

David writes in Psalm 1:1-3: *"**BLESSED** is the man that walketh not in the counsel of the ungodly, nor standeth in the way of sinners, nor sitteth in the seat of the scornful. But his delight is in the law of the LORD: And in his law doth he meditate day and night.*

And he shall be like a tree planted by the rivers of water, that bringeth forth his fruit in his season: his leaf also shall not wither; and whatsoever he doeth shall prosper."

Chapter Three: Debt Destruction – Strategy and Tactic

Moses writes in the book of Deuteronomy, chapter 28, verses 12, 43 & 44: ***"Thee LORD shall open unto thee his good treasure, the heaven to give the rain upon thy land in his season, and to bless all the work of thine hand: thou shalt lend unto many nations, and thou shalt not borrow."*** (This is just a small part of the blessing of God.)

"The stranger that is within thee shall get up above very high; and thou shalt come down very low. He shall lend unto thee, and thou shalt not lend unto him: he shall be the head, and thou shalt be the tail." This is living under the, **'spirit of poverty.'**

Strategy and Tactic

What do I mean by Strategy and Tactic? 'Strategy' is your **overall plan** for demolishing your debts. Whereas, 'Tactic' is **the technique** you will employ to bring about this desired result.

First, you must **develop an overall plan** to destroy your debts and secondly, you must **develop a technique** to carry out your plan.

(1) The word, **strategy** is derived from two Greek words, **'stratos'** which means **an army,** and the Greek word, **'agein'** which means, **to lead. Your overall plan**

then is to lead your army in the battle against your debts in order to wipe them completely out!

(2) The word, **Tactic** is derived from the Greek phrase, **'he takike techne'** which means, **the art or science of arranging troops for battle.**

Let us read the following Scriptures:

"For which of you, intending to build a tower, sitteth not down first, and counteth the cost, whether he have sufficient to finish it. Lest haply, after he hath laid the foundation, and is not able to finish it, all that behold it begin to mock him saying, This man began to build, but was not able to finish.

Or what king, going to make war against another king, sitteth not down first, and consulteth whether he be able with ten thousand to meet him that cometh against him with twenty thousand? Or else, while the other is yet a great way off, he sendeth an ambassage, and desireth conditions of peace." Luke 14:28-32

"The rich ruleth over the poor, and the borrower is servant to the lender." Prov. 2:7

Chapter Three: Debt Destruction – Strategy and Tactic

Sitting Down and Counting the Cost

Concerning your debts, you must know: **where you are, what your present position is, how great is your desire for the destruction of your debts and what are you willing to do to get out of debt.**

Up till now, 'Debt' has been your master and you have been its slave. Yes, a slave, a slave to the **'spirit of poverty,'** a cruel master indeed. It is time for you to rebel. It is time for you to say, 'enough.' It is time for you to go to war and fight against your enemy---DEBT---and free yourself from its bondage.

Knowing Where You Are and What Your Present Financial Condition Is

To accomplish this, you need to sit down now and compile **two lists.**

One that shows **exactly what you owe.** The other that shows **exactly what you own.**

When you have completed these two lists, you will have a clear understanding of your present financial condition. With this information in hand, you are in a position to manage your finances in a way that will serve you and not dictate to you. You will become the master and not the servant. The more exact you are with these two lists the more powerful will be your **'war on debt.'**

Use it or Sell it

Now make a third list entitled: **'The Things I Must Sell.'**

This list will contain three columns: (i) **'Item Description,'** (ii) **'Original Cost,'** and (iii) **'Selling Price.'** (You will use the proceeds from the sales in your **'war on debt.'**

You are now ready for the eradication of your debts! So get all excited!

The Strategy for Debt Destruction

I want you to **imagine** each dollar – **of the eight tenths*** of your earnings – as **'a soldier' in your army over which you are the General.** Each soldier in your army is ready, willing and waiting for you to send him out to fight and destroy your enemy----**DEBT.**

Your initial campaign in this warfare is to cease looking at your bills as many bills, but rather look on them as **ONE LARGE BILL!**

Chapter Three: Debt Destruction – Strategy and Tactic

Secondly, you must do the same with your monthly payments. Instead of looking at them as many payments, you must look upon them as **ONE GIANT PAYMENT!**

Your overall strategy or plan is simply this: while your **ONE LARGE BILL** will become less each month when a smaller bill is paid off, your **GIANT MONTHLY PAYMENT WILL REMAIN THE SAME!**

*One tenth is the Lord's Tithe. The other tenth is yours to keep. More will be said about this later.

The Tactic for Eliminating Your Debts

Target for Destruction:

Focus on the bill which will be paid in full in the shortest amount of time. Let us suppose its monthly payment is $80. When this bill is paid off **YOU ARE NOT GOING TO HAVE AN EXTRA $80 TO SPEND.** Instead, you are going to have **$80 extra to target the next bill for elimination!**

This may not of necessity be the bill with the fewest payments. Choose one with the higher interest amount and target that one for destruction. This may take a little more time, but adding that extra $80 to the monthly payment will mean that you will have a greater amount of money to apply to the next bill (targeted for elimination) after that one is paid off. You will use the money from the sale of goods to aid you in this debt reduction strategy and tactic.

Finally, pay off your car. Remember, all payments on your other bills – including the car payment – that the extra amount of money added to your payments must be **APPLIED AGAINST THE PRINCIPLE.** (Home Mortgage payments are dealt with in Chapter 5.)

As a believer, go to the Lord in prayer and boldly ask Him for a miracle of, **'Debt Release.'**

A principle that was revealed to me by God some years ago was this: **tithes on your debts.**

I was sitting in a service in Hawaii waiting to minister God's Word to the people when the Spirit of God whispered in my heart, **"Tell the people to tithe on their debts and I will double the amount back to them that they are in debt for."** I began to pray in heart, "Lord, do you want me to share this with these people now or is it for a later time?"

I had no sooner prayed this prayer than a lady pastor in the service jumped to her feet and explained. "The Lord has just spoken to me and said, 'I want you to be debt free,' but I don't know how." I had my answer. I stood and shared with the congregation what the Lord had whispered in my heart. I gave the following example. "Let us suppose that your debts $8,000. The tithe on this amount is $800. Now you don't have $800, so how do you tithe on this debt? Each week, just add whatever you can afford to your tithes and mark it, 'Tithe on debt.' I closed by saying, "When I return in two weeks time I know we will hear testimonies of what the Lord has done."

Two weeks later I returned to Honolulu from one of the outer islands. I was met at the baggage terminal by one of the pastors. She said to me, "Brother Coady, when my husband died I was left with hospital charges of just over $8,000. Each month I have sent a small amount to reduce the debt. I took to heart what you told us about tithing on our debts and began that night. Here is a letter I just received from the Hospital Board. Please read it." Her face revealed nothing of its contents. I took the letter out of the envelope and began to read:

"Dear Mrs.---

At the annual meeting of the Board we were looking over the outstanding balances of accounts owed to the hospital. Your account came before the Board and we took note that you have consistent endeavored to reduce this bill. Because of this, it was the unanimous decision of the Board to cancel the remaining debt. You now owe the Hospital nothing."

We stood together in the baggage terminal area praising, thanking, and blessing God.

God is no respecter of persons. What He has done for others, He will do for you. Jesus said: *"Ask, and it shall be given you. For everyone that asketh receiveth."* Matt. 7:7&8.

(See Appendix I for a Biblical example of "Miracle Debt Destruction.")

Chapter Four

The Third Building Block
Watch Your Savings Grow

"And God blessed them, saying, be fruitful and multiply." Genesis 1:22

"And God blessed them, and God said unto them, Be fruitful, and multiply, and replenish the earth, and subdue it and have dominion…" Genesis 1:28

"The blessing of the LORD, it maketh rich, and he addeth no sorrow with it." Proverbs 10:22

"And Abram was very rich in...silver and gold." Genesis 13:2

"And when...thy silver and gold is multiplied, and all that thou hast is multiplied...thou shalt remember the LORD thy God: for it is he that giveth thee power to get wealth, that he may establish his covenant which he sware unto thy fathers." Deuteronomy 8:13 & 20

"The rich man's wealth is his strong city: the destruction of the poor is their poverty." Proverbs 10:15

"Bless the LORD, O my soul, and forget not all his benefits...Who redeemeth thy life from destruction." Psalm 103 2&4

"Acquaint now thyself with him, and be at peace: thereby good shall come unto thee. Receive, I pray thee, the law from his mouth, and lay up his words in thine heart.

If thou return to the Almighty, thou shalt be built up, thou shalt put away iniquity far from thy tabernacles. Then shalt thou lay up gold as dust, and the gold of Ophir as the stones of the brooks. Yea, the

Chapter Four: Watch Your Savings Grow

Almighty shall be thy defense, and thou shalt have plenty of silver.

For then thou shalt have thy delight n the Almighty, and shalt lift up thy face unto God. Thou shalt make thy prayer unto him, and he shall hear thee, and thou shalt pay thy vows.

Thou shalt also decree a thing, and it shall be established unto thee: and the light shall shine upon thy ways." Job 22:21-28

It is time to start your savings to multiplying. The one-tenth that you have set aside from your earnings is but the beginning. The earnings it will make are what will build your fortune.

Your personal wealth consists not in the dollars you carry in your wallet; **it is the income that you will build with them. A STREAM OF SILVER AND GOLD THAT CONTINUALLY FLOWS INTO YOUR BILLFOLD AND KEEPS IT BULGING TO OVERFLOWING.**

From your meager earnings you can give birth to a hoard of golden and silver bondservants. Each one at your command, laboring and earning for you more wealth. As they work for you they will beget more children and they will beget other children until, through their combined efforts your income will multiply and increase. This is a God-ordained principle – **everything produces after its kind.**

"And God said, Let the earth bring forth grass and herb yielding seed, and the fruit tree yielding fruit after his kind, whose seed is in itself, upon the earth, and it was so.

And the earth brought forth grass, and herb yielding seed after his kind, and the tree yielding fruit, whose seed was in itself, after his kind: and God saw that it was good." Genesis 1:11-12

How is this accomplished? The one-tenth which you have set aside from your earnings (not the Lord's Tithe) should have been put initially into a Savings Account even though this only yields a small interest rate. However, a little is better than nothing.

Each dollar must now be sent out of this account to labor for you and reproduce after its kind according to God's ordained principle. This can be accomplished in a variety of ways:

(1) Certificates of Deposits (CDs). The interest ate is higher than a savings account and varies from three months to twenty years. I personally choose three months and then renew for another three months.

(2) US Savings Bonds. These yield a higher interest and should be kept in a safety deposit box at your bank or at home in a fireproof safe.

(3) US Government Bonds, which yield a higher interest rate again. (Foreign Governments invest in these bonds, so why shouldn't you?)

(4) State Government Bonds, which yield a high interest rate.

(5) Municipal Bonds, which also yield a high interest rate.

Your Federal, State and local taxes are used to pay off these Bonds, so why shouldn't you enjoy some of the benefits of your taxes?

Finally, **long term investments,** e.g., Mutual Funds, the Stock Market, Commodities, etc. However, these should not be undertaken without the wise advice of a trust Investment Counselor. **Proceed slowly and cautiously in this area.**

WARNING! DANGER! PRECIPICE AHEAD!

BEWARE of get-rich-quick schemes, no matter how good they sound and regardless of who advises you to invest in them. <u>Hold on to your hard-earned money and invest wisely.</u>

Remember, the old saying, 'If it sounds too good to be true---it is!' Another old English proverb says, 'A fool and his money are soon parted!'

Your gold and silver bondservants are now laboring for you, multiplying and producing after their kind. They are serving you in bringing you an income – a stream of wealth flowing into your storehouse – your bank account.

"Blessed shall be thy basket and thy store." **Deuteronomy 28:5** Your basket is your billfold.

"The LORD shall command the blessing upon thee in thy storehouses, and in all that thou settest thine hand unto." **Deuteronomy 28:8**

A. Ronald Coady

Chapter Five

The Fourth Building Block
Guard Your Savings from Loss
The Law of Teaching – Repetition

Let us reiterate what we have taught in the previous chapters.

Misfortune loves a shining mark. Your savings must be guarded with diligence or you will lose them.

First, you must secure small amounts of money and learn to protect it before God will entrust you with larger amounts.

The initial sound principle of investment is security for your savings, which is your capital.

Before parking with your savings, study carefully and be fully assured that your capital can be safely reclaimed when you need it. **Remember, the penalty of risk is usually loss!** Once again, remember to avoid like the plague, 'get rich quick schemes.' Do not be misled by romantic desires of gaining wealth rapidly. That is a sign of greed. The Apostle Paul warns us, ***"For the love of money is the root of all evil: which while some coveted after, they have erred from the faith, and pierced themselves through with many sorrows."*** I Timothy 6:10. The devil didn't do it. They did it to themselves.

Second, guard your savings from loss by investing only where your capital is **safe.** Only where you can reclaim it when needed and where you will not fail to collect a fair rental fee (interest) on your money. **You are now the lender and not the borrower.** You are renting out your money to those institutions where you invest it and they are paying you a rental fee – interest on your loan to them.

Chapter Five: Guard Your Savings From Loss

Third, consult with wise people. Secure advice from those experienced in the profitable handling of money. Let their wisdom protect your savings from unsafe investments.

"Where no counsel is, the people fall: but in the multitude of counselors there is safety." Proverbs 11:14.

"Strong men retain riches." Proverbs 11:16

A. Ronald Coady

Chapter Six

The Fifth Building Block
Protecting Your Children's Inheritance

"But if any provide not for his own, especially for those of his own house, he hath denied the faith, and is worse than an infidel." I Timothy 5:8

"A good man leaveth an inheritance to his children's children."

"For the children should not lay up for the parents, but the parents for the children."
II Corinthians 12:14

"House and riches are the inheritance of fathers."
Proverbs 19:14

In 1967 when I was ministering in Vancouver, British Columbia, the senior pastor asked me, "What provision have you made for your family is you suddenly die?" I replied with a religious answer, "We believe that the Lord will return soon and so I am not concerned about this." To which he responded, "What if He doesn't return soon and you die, what provision have you made for your family?" My response to this was, "The church, which I pastor, will take care of them." He blurted out – rather angrily – "Your church will do no such thing! Furthermore, it is not your church's responsibility, but ours!" He then quoted the verse above, I Timothy 5:8.

His statement hit me like a cannonball in the chest. I asked him how I should do this and he proceeded to instruct me. I look back on that conversation as a watershed in my life.

Setting Your House in Order

"Thus saith the LORD, Set thine house in order; for thou shalt die, and not live." II Kings 20:1

"Hear counsel, and receive instruction, that thou mayest be wise in thy latter end." Proverbs 19:20

If Jesus does not return in our lifetime, it is an irrefutable fact, **we shall all die.** It is important, therefore, that our households are set in order before this event. If you died today or tomorrow would you die with your house in order? If not, why?

Perform each of the following instructions and your house will be set in order. Then you and your loved

Chapter Six: Protecting Your Children's Inheritance

ones can rest assured that all is well should you die before Jesus returns.

Insurance Policies

LIFE INSURANCE

One of the first things you should do is take out Life Insurance policies on you, your wife, and your children. These policies should be for no less than $50,000 each and should include a double indemnity clause. Ensure that the policies are taken out with an Insurance Company that is a reputable and well-established firm. Also, that is has a high track record for honoring and paying out on claims. The younger you are when you take out these policies the lower will be your monthly premiums.

LONG-TERM HEALTH CARE INSURANCE

A Long-Term Health Care Insurance Policy should be taken out on you, your spouse, and children. This is a safeguard for your assets and savings against any catastrophic illness which may strike you or your family. Again, the younger you are when you take out this kind of policy the lower will be your monthly premiums.

BURIAL INSURANCE

Unless Jesus returns we will all die. We should therefore make provision for our death and disposal of our last remains. We do this in order that the surviving members of our family will not be burdened with this expense. Consult with your local Funeral Home Director. He will advise you of various plans that you can take out.

Make sure that all your Insurance Policies are kept in a safe place and are easily accessible when needed, either in a safety deposit box at a bank or in a fireproof safe at home.

OWNING YOUR OWN HOME

God has promised, *"They shall sit every man under his vine and under his fig tree: and none shall make them afraid."* Micah 4:4

This is a Biblical euphemism for owning and enjoying your own home and property.

"Jesus answered and said, 'Verily I say unto you, There is no man that hath left house, or brethren, or sisters, or father, or mother, or wife, or children, or lands, for my sake and the gospel. But he shall receive an hundredfold now in this time, houses and brethren and sisters and mothers, and children and lands, with persecutions; and in the world to come eternal life.'" Mark 10:29-30

Chapter Six: Protecting Your Children's Inheritance

BUYING YOUR OWN HOME

Very few people are blessed with inheriting a house and property. Each family needs its own place they can call home. Paying rent on a house is a fool's game. It is putting your hard earned cash into someone else's pocket. So why not put it in your own? T may be necessary for a short period of time to rent a house or apartment. This should only be a temporary arrangement. **The end in view is always to own your own home. Your home is your most profitable investment.** It is not beyond the ability of any well-intentioned person to own his or her own home.

The house you choose to buy should be one that will meet your everyday needs, **not** your wants. This is important. You do not want a millstone around your neck for twenty-five to thirty years.

PROCEDURE FOR BUYING A HOUSE

Once you have found the house you wish to purchase, (this is usually done through a Real Estate Agency), you will be required to put down a deposit of approximately 5% of the purchase price.

Go to your bank or credit union and apply for a Home Real Estate Loan for the balance and add the amount of the closing costs to this loan application for the maximum amount of time, say, thirty years. In doing this, your monthly payments will be lower than a fifteen year loan. **Do not agree to a final balloon payment. That is not to your advantage.** Take out an additional loan called a "Home Mortgage Insurance Policy." The monthly payment on this policy will be added to your monthly house payments. This is to ensure that if through some unforeseen catastrophe you are unable to make your monthly loan payments, they will be made through your Home Mortgage Insurance Policy while you are incapacitated. Thus, your home is safe.

The day your loan is approved, and **this is most important** (have your checkbook with you) and after you sign the Loan papers, go to the nearest bank teller and make your first house payment with the Loan Payment number on the face of your check. The bank will protest vigorously, but insist on making this payment anyway.

Why should you do this? **Not until you draw against these funds in purchasing your home does any interest accrue!** In making the first house payment the day the loan is funded you will reduce the length of time the loan is to be paid by three years or more. That is why the bank will vigorously protest. Remember, banks make their money on the interest that is paid on loans.

You have no moved into your new home. I will show you now how to reduce that thirty year mortgage to ten to fifteen years. Impossible? No. This is how is it accomplished.

Your bank may have issued you with a monthly payment book. **Whatever you do, DO NOT – I reiterate, DO NOT – opt to make your monthly house payments through automatic withdrawal, unless it is to your benefit.** (Although some banks will offer a small percentage for auto payments.) The reason for this will be obvious in a moment. If you study your monthly coupons you will find a space that will read, **'Principle'.** You are going to add an extra amount of money to this part of your monthly house payment.

Let us suppose that your monthly payment is $1,200. You are going to add to you payment 1% of this amount, which is $12. You will identify that $12 amount in the **'Principle'** box on the coupon. Your total monthly payment is then $1,212. You will do this for the first year. Write the same information on the memo section of your check – Monthly Payment, $1,200; Principle $12 = $1,212.

The second year you will increase your monthly payment by 2% ($24) and follow the same procedure as above. The third year you will increase the amount by 3%. The fourth year by 4% and so on. By the time you reach the tenth year your mortgage should be paid off. It not, it almost will be. I suggested in Chapter 2 that the money you have saved through the elimination of your debts be applied to other debts. It is time to use that money in paying off the **'Principle'** on your Home Mortgage Loan. Just follow the steps above.

Do not be concerned if your Mortgage Loan Agreement **includes an early payment penalty clause.** It is worth paying the penalty and save at least well over $100,000 or more. What most homeowners do not realize is that by the time they pay off their mortgage, using the least payment the bank calls for, **THEY HAVE PAID FOR THEIR HOME SEVERAL TIMES OVER!** Remember, banks make their money on the interest you pay them. On the average home loan all you have been paying for about ten years is **INTEREST.** It will be years before you have built up any equity in your home. (It is the same with automobile loans.)

Now to conclude this section:

A LAST WILL AND TESTAMENT
OR
A REVOCABLE FAMILY TRUST?

Most people have a Last Will and Testament, and this is good. However, upon the death of the last testator, that Will and Testament must be probated by the Court. This will involve Attorney Fees, Court Fees and, depending on the size of your estate, Inheritance

Chapter Six: Protecting Your Children's Inheritance

Taxes. All of these costs can be avoided through forming a Revocable Family Trust!

The laws governing Family Trusts differ from state to state and from county to county, so it is important that you engage the services of a reputable attorney who specializes in Estate Planning and Family Trusts. It will be worth it.

What are the advantages of a Family Trust? Many. Upon the death of either spouse the surviving spouse becomes the sole Trustee. The surviving spouse than appoints Successor Trustees and, upon his or her death, the Trust carries on. There is no probating of the Will, Court costs, Attorney Fees, or Inheritance Taxes. Your family may enjoy the full benefits of your hard earned money.

When you Family Trust is formed all Real Estate, Bank Accounts, Insurance Policies, CDs, Savings Certificates, Stock and Bonds, Retirement Accounts will be transferred into the Name of the Family Trust. The Title Deeds of your home and car will also be transferred to the Trust. Your bank or financial institution may hold your title deeds, but this will not affect the Name Change.

Another advantage of a Family Trust is that should you suffer some catastrophic illness and your insurance coverage runs out, all your assets are safe and cannot be seized to pay the bills incurred. Some people have lost home, savings and everything they owned to pay hospital and other bills because of catastrophic illness.

In May 1989, Muriel and I formed a Revocable Family Trust. When she died in June 1998, I became the surviving Trustee. Later, I appointed my son and daughter as my Successor Trustees. Regardless of what may happen in the future, my children and their children and their children's children's inheritance is safe. The peace of mind that this brings is worth more than can be imagined.

WHAT A FAMILY TRUST CONSISTS OF

When you form your Family Trust, it could be a rather lengthy document. The preamble will look something like this:

ESTATE PLAN FOR
(Your Surname) **FAMILY TRUST**

Binder Index

Description of Document

<u>**No.**</u>   <u>**Date**</u>

   1.   **Chart Illustrating Estate Planning**

Chapter Six: Protecting Your Children's Inheritance

2. (Name) **Family Trust by**(You and your spouse's full names)
3. **Certified Extract of trust**
4. **General Transfer**
5. **Will of** (Your full name)
6. **Will of** (Your spouse's full name)
7. **Durable Power of Attorney for** (a family member or trusted friend)
8. **Durable power of Attorney for** (a family member or trusted friend) (The need for two Powers of Attorney is that if one is incapacitated, the other can step in.)
9. **Durable Power of Attorney for Health Care for** (Your full name)
10. **Durable Power of Attorney for Health Care for (**Your spouses full name)
11. **Appointment of Co-Trustees of the** (Name) **Family Trust**

If your children are under age you will need to appoint trusted Guardians for them in the event that you both die, are killed in an accident, or are totally incapacitated to care for them. Solomon tells us, ***"There be just men, unto whom it happeneth according to the work of the wicked; again, there be wicked men to whom it happeneth according to the work of the righteous." Ecclesiastes 8:14.*** In other words, bad things happen to good people and good things happen to bad people. Provide against this possibility.

There you have it – All the vital information to set your house and your affairs in order.

DON'T DELAY – DO IT TODAY

PROCRASTINATION IS THE THIEF OF TIME

Chapter Seven

The Sixth Building Block
Insuring You Have a Future Income

"Hear counsel, and receive instruction, that thou mayest be wise in thy latter end." Proverbs 19:19

"Poverty and shame shall be to him that refuseth instruction: but he that regardeth reproof shall be honoured." Proverbs 13:18

"In the house of the righteous there is much treasure: but in the revenues of the wicked is trouble." Proverbs 15:6

"He that gathereth in summer is a wise son: but he that sleepeth in harvest is a son that causeth shame." Proverbs 10:5

Each person's life proceeds from childhood to old age. Therefore, it is incumbent upon each of us to prepare for that time.

1. We must make sure that we have prepared a suitable income for the time when we are no longer young.

2. We must ensure that our family is suitable provided for when we are no longer able to be with them to comfort, uphold, and strengthen them.

Everyone who understands the principles for accumulating wealth, i.e., how to acquire a growing surplus, must give thought to those future days. To do so you should plan investments and or provision that will safely endure for many years, yet will be available when the time arrives which you have anticipated and wisely provided for.

Chapter Seven: Insuring You Have a Future Income

There are many diverse ways by which you may safely provide for your future old age and retirement. There are IRA Accounts, KEOGHS, etc. Your accountant or financial advisor will be able to counsel you about a suitable Retirement Plan to meet your needs.

No matter how prosperous your business or investments are today, **you must afford to insure a good income for your future old age and protection of your family.**

We live in our own day and times and not in the future. So we must take advantage of those means and ways which will accomplish our purposes for the future. Therefore, we must be wise and with well though-out methods to provide against want and poverty in our senior years.

A. Ronald Coady

Chapter Eight

The Seventh Building Block
Increasing Your Ability to Learn and Earn

"The desire of the righteous shall be granted." Proverbs 10:24

"The desire of the righteous is only good." Proverbs 11:23

"But when the desire cometh it is a tree of life." Proverbs 13:12

"The desire accomplished is sweet to the soul." Proverbs 13:19

"Delight thyself also in the LORD; and he shall give thee the desires of thine heart." Psalm 37:4

Preceding all accomplishment is **DESIRE**. **Your desires must be strong and definite.** Most people's desires are so general that they amount to nothing more than weak longings.

Merely wishing to accumulate wealth is of little purpose, but to **DESIRE** to have $500 in the bank is a **TANGIBLE DESIRE** which you can press forward with and accomplish. After you have fulfilled your **DESIRE** for $500, you will find similar ways and means to increase it by $1,000, and then to multiply that amount many times over!

In learning to secure your **ONE SMALL DEFINITE DESIRE** you have **disciplined** and **trained** yourself to secure a larger one. This is the process by which a personal fortune is built; **first in small amounts,** then into larger sums as you learn and become more capable to earn.

How To Form Desires

All **DESIRES** begin with a **thought.** You begin by **thinking** about your immediate goal.

Next, you use your faculty of **imagination.** Imagination is the **"eye of faith."** You **see** your goal attained. You **see** that $500 in your hand. You **see** yourself banking it into your Savings Account.

Chapter Eight: Increasing Your Ability to Learn and Earn

Now you begin to affirm it with a loud voice, **"I have $500 and I am banking it in my Savings Account."** You confess this over and over as your form the **mental picture** of it in your mind. Do this last thing at night before you go to sleep and first thing upon waking in the morning. Your subconscious mind will take over the image and by some strange alchemy, we don't know how, it will form **DESIRE** and produce **faith**, by which all things become possible. Jesus said, *"All things are possible to him that believeth."* Mark 9:23 Again, He said, *"Nothing shall be impossible unto you."* Matthew 17:20

Faith is an attitude of heart and mind which may be produced at will.

DESIRE combined with **will power** produced the necessary **action** to bring about your desired result. This is a God-ordained principle that you may exercise at will.

PERFRECTING YOUR SKILLS

"When the wise is instructed, he receiveth knowledge." Proverbs 21:11

"Poverty and shame shall be to him that refuseth instruction." Proverbs 13:18

"Give instruction to a wise man and he will be yet wiser: teach a just man, and he will increase in learning." Proverbs 9:9

"Do you see a man skilled in his work? He will serve before kings; he will not serve before obscure men." Proverbs 22:29 (NIV Translation)

As you perfect yourself in your work, your ability to earn will increase. The more knowledge and wisdom you acquire about your employment, the more will be your earning capacity. The person who seeks to become more skillful in their trade will be more than amply rewarded.

Keen minded people seek greater skill in their jobs so that they may be of better service to those who employ them and upon whom they depend for their earnings.

It is essential that you learn not only to respect others but you must develop self-respect. To do this you **must:**

1. Pay your debts promptly. Purchasing only that for which you are able to pay. (No more charging on Charge Cards or Credit Cards unless absolutely necessary.)

2. Take good care of your family and spend quality time with them. Show an interest in their everyday affairs. Encourage them in their dreams and pursuits.

Chapter Eight: Increasing Your Ability to Learn and Earn

3. Be generous – within reasonable limits – to those who encounter misfortune. Assist them as you would want others to assist you if you were in the same circumstances. *"He that hath pity on the poor lendeth to the LORD; and that which he hath given will he pay him again."* Proverbs 19:17

4. Cultivate your ability to study in order to become wiser and more skillful in your place of employment and act respectfully to others and yourself. Remember the admonition of the greatest of all teachers, our Lord Jesus Christ, who instructed us saying*, "All things whatsoever ye would that men should do to you, do ye even so to them."* Matthew 7:12

5. Learn more about your job by taking courses to improve your skills. Knowledge is never a burden to carry; it may be a burden to attain, but once you have it you will have it always.

Well, there you have it. Know **what**, know **how**, and understand **why.**

Remember: We Are Surrounded By Wealth Beyond Our Wildest Dreams

There Is An Overabundance For All

A. Ronald Coady

APPENDIX I

Miracle Debt Cancellation

The classic example of **"Miracle Debt Cancellation"** is found in the story of the children of Israel's deliverance from Egyptian bondage. The story is recorded in the book of Exodus chapters eleven through thirteen.

Over four hundred years before this event, God spoke to Abram. He told him, ***"Know of a surety that thy seed shall be a stranger in a land that is not theirs, and shall serve them; and they shall afflict them four hundred years: And also that nation, whom they serve, will I judge: and afterward shall they come out with great substance."*** Genesis 15:13-14

When the time of their deliverance came, God appeared to Moses in the Burning Bush. He commanded him to bring Israel out of the house of bondage. He informed him saying, ***"I will give this people favour in the sight of the Egyptians: and it shall come to pass, that*** *when ye go, ye shall not go empty: But every woman shall BORROW of her neighbour, and of her that sojourneth in her house, jewels of silver, and jewels of gold, and raiment: and ye shall put them upon your sons, and upon your daughters; and ye shall spoil the Egyptians."* Exodus 3:22-23 (Emphasis mine.)

The record continues, *"And the children of Israel did according to the word of Moses; and they BORROWED of the Egyptians jewels of silver, and jewels of gold, and raiment: And the LORD gave the people favour in the sight of the Egyptians, so that they LENT unto them such things as they required. And they spoiled the Egyptians."* Exodus 12:35-36. (The emphasis of the words 'borrowed and lent' is mine.)

Now, when we borrow something and the party we borrow from lends it to us, it is understood clearly that we will return all borrowed items. Otherwise we would be thieves.

Pharaoh had entered into an agreement with God, Moses, and the children of Israel. The agreement was this, *"The LORD God of the Hebrews hath met with us: and now let us go, we beseech thee, three days journey into the wilderness, that we may sacrifice unto the LORD our God."*

Appendix I: Miracle Debt Cancellation

Only after God plagued Pharaoh, his household, his servants, and all the Egyptians did he agree to God's terms. The children of Israel were to go three days journey into the wilderness and sacrifice to the Lord. It is obvious that Pharaoh's understanding of the agreement was that after they accomplished sacrificing to the Lord in the wilderness, Israel would return to Egypt. Everything they had borrowed from the Egyptians would then be returned to the lenders.

The children of Israel had an enormous debt to repay. If they did not return and repay the loan then they would be a nation of thieves. What a dilemma. Let us see now how God performed a **"Miracle of Debt Cancellation.**

It is a well-known fact that when two parties enter into a binding agreement and one party reneges on their obligation as stated in the agreement, the other party is not bound to perform their obligation as agreed.

After the people left Egypt – every one of them were multi-millionaires – Pharaoh reneged on his obligation as agreed. *"And it was told the king of Egypt that the people fled: and the heart of Pharaoh and of his servants was turned against the people, and they said, Why have we done this, that we have let Israel go from serving us?...But the Egyptians pursued after them."* Exodus 14:5 & 9

Pharaoh had broken the agreement. Israel is no longer bound to fulfill its part of the agreement. Nothing borrowed by Israel or lent to them needs to be returned.

The king and his armies pursued them before they had gone three days into the wilderness. The three days journey into the wilderness had not yet begun. God brought His people to the Red Sea. The Egyptians caught up with them. The waters of the Red Sea were miraculously parted and Israel crossed over on dry ground into the wilderness. Pharaoh's endeavor to pursue them through the sea – determined to bring them back – is divinely thwarted. At the command of God, the parted waters return to their natural state, drowning the Egyptian army and their chariots in the sea. *"The sea covered them: they sank like lead in the mighty waters."* Exodus 15:10

God Canceled The Debt – Israel Is Debt Free

The Psalmist triumphantly sings, *"He brought them forth also with silver and gold: and there was not one feeble person among their tribes…He brought forth his people with joy, and his chosen with gladness."* Psalm 105:37 & 42

The apostle Paul wrote, with particular reference to this event, *"Now all these things happened unto them*

Appendix I: Miracle Debt Cancellation

for ensamples: and they are written for our admonition upon whom the ends of the world are come." I Corinthians 10:11

Believe God for your 'Miracle Debt Cancellation.'

A. Ronald Coady

APPENDIX II

The Lord's Portion Tithes & Offerings

"For them that honour me I will honour." I Samuel 2:30

During the time of the Second Temple, God says to His people, *"A son honoureth his father, and a servant his master; if I then be a father, where is mine honour? And if I be a master, where is my fear? Saith the LORD of hosts."* Malachi 1:6

"Honour the LORD with thy substance, and with the first fruits of all thing increase: So shall thy barns be filled with plenty, and thy presses shall burst out with new wine." Proverbs 3:9-10

Honoring God with our substance is giving Him our tithes. Honoring him with our first fruits is giving Him offerings.

The Lord's Tithe

Ten percent of all you earn belongs to the Lord. *"**All the tithes of the land, whether of the seed of the land, or the fruit of the tree, is the LORD'S: it is holy unto the LORD…whatsoever passeth under thy rod, the tenth shall be holy unto the LORD.**"* Leviticus 27:30 & 32

God says a tenth of everything you earn belongs to Him and is holy unto Him. We are to tithe off the gross amount, **not the net amount.** A tenth of whatsoever 'passeth under' your rod God has declared to be holy unto Him.

Some may object, "Well that was under the Law, but we are not under the Law but under Grace." This is true, that we are under Grace and not the Law. However, although tithing was incorporated under the Law, it did not originate with the Law but under Grace and the Promise. Tithing begins with Abram when he meets Melchizedek, God's King-Priest.

*"**And Melchizedek king of Salem brought forth bread and wine: and he was priest of the most high God. And he blessed him and said, Blessed be Abram of the most high God, possessor of heaven and earth: And blessed be the most high God, which hath delivered thine enemies into thy hand. And he gave him tithes of all." Genesis 14:18-20***

Appendix II: The Lord's Portion - Tithes and Offerings

It is significant to note that Abram tithes to Melchizedek while still in uncircumcision, and also before his faith is accounted to him for righteousness. This attests to the fact that tithing is not for the Jew only, but also for the Gentiles.

Paul, the apostle, interprets this incident in the life of Abraham in his epistle to the Hebrews, ***"For this Melchisedec, king of Salem, priest of the most high God, who met Abraham returning from the slaughter of the kings, and blessed him. To whom you also Abraham gave a tenth part of all; first being by interpretation King of righteousness, and after that also King of Salem, which is King of peace."*** Hebrews 7:1-2

As you read the rest of this chapter, he teaches us that Jesus is made a High priest after the order of Melchizedek. ***"The Lord sware and will not repent, thou art a priest for ever after the order of Melchisedec."*** Hebrews 7:21

The Greek word for the English word, 'order' is "taxis,' which means 'arrangement.' The Lord Jesus, our High Priest, is a priest after the 'arrangement' of the Melchizedek priesthood. What is that arrangement?

1. **Ministering the bread and the wine – the Holy Communion;**

2. The giving and receiving of tithes, and

3. Blessing.

It is apparent that tithing is as much a basic fundamental of the Christian Dispensation as Blessing and Holy Communion are.

Because we are now the children of Abraham, we walk in the **'steps of the faith of Abraham.'** *"That he might be the father of all them that believe, though they be not circumcised; that righteousness might be imputed unto them also: And the father of the circumcision to them who are not of the circumcision only, but who also walk in the steps of that faith of our father Abraham, which he had being yet uncircumcised."* Romans 4:11-12

We tithe because we are walking in the steps of the faith of our father Abraham. Following his example, we bring our tithes to our heavenly High Priest, Jesus our Melchizedek, from whose hands we receive the 'bread and the wine', which are the communion of His Body and Blood. We respond by worshipping Him with our tithes and offerings. He blesses us and makes us possessors of heaven and earth as He, Himself, is.

Appendix II: The Lord's Portion - Tithes and Offerings

God Challenges Us To Tithe

The Lord speaking through the prophet Malachi, challenges His people. ***"Will a man rob God? Yet have ye robbed me. But ye say, wherein have we robbed thee? In tithes and offerings.***

Ye are cursed wit ha curse: for ye have robbed me, even this whole nation.

Bring ye all the tithes into the storehouse, that there may be meat in mine house, and prove me now herewith, saith the LORD of hosts, if I will not open you the windows o heaven, and pour you out a blessing, that there shall not be room enough to receive it. And I will rebuke the devourer for your sakes." Malachi 3:8-12

Let it be perfectly clear, **God does not need our money,** but we need to give. Tithing is only the beginning, not the end all. Tithing is basically a teacher.

We are to bring our tithes to **the 'storehouse.'** The storehouse is the ministry which feeds us with the Word of God. We tithe to the Lord. The Lord has designated those tithes for the support of the ministry.

"The tithes of the children of Israel, which they offer as an heave offering unto the LORD, I have

given to the Levites to inherit: therefore, I have said unto them, Among the children of Israel they shall have no inheritance." Numbers 18:24

The Levites tithed on these tithes and their tithe was to be given to Aaron the High Priest.

"Thus speak unto the Levites, and say unto them, When ye take of the tithes of the children of Israel the tithes which I have given you from them for your inheritance, then ye shall offer up an heave offering of it for the LORD, even a tenth part of the tithe…Thus shall ye offer an heave offering unto the LORD of all your tithes, which ye receive from the children of Israel; and ye shall give thereof the LORD's heave offering to Aaron the priest." Numbers 18:26 & 28

The tithes which we bring to the House of the Lord on the Lord's Day, at the Lord's Table, are to be given to the ministry for its support. They are not the property of the Church Board. They are not under the disposition of the Church Treasurer to be dispensed for the paying of the Church's mortgage, bills, etc. The ministry may use the tithes for this purpose, but that is at its discretion.

Appendix II: The Lord's Portion - Tithes and Offerings

Bring Ye All The Tithes Into The Storehouse

The Lord charges us to bring all our tithes into the storehouse, not to send them. We do not send our tithes to an evangelist, a missionary, etc. We do not put them into a visiting minister's love offering. To do so would be to make that person a **"receiver of stolen goods."** They are **not** our tithes; they are the Lord's Tithe, His portion which He ahs designated for his ministers.

An Analogy

When I am teaching on the subject of **'Tithing,'** I use the following analogy.

When Abraham gave his tithes to Melchizedek he was honoring the most high God as Possessor of heaven and earth (the Property Owner of heaven and earth.) In other words, he was paying his rent to his landlord.

When we rent an apartment or house, the property owner, the landlord, is responsible for all major repairs – as long as we are not responsible for the damage. Usually he appoints an agent to collect his rent money. Let us suppose there is a problem with the plumbing. We call the landlord and/or his manager and make our complaint. If we have been lax in paying the rent or are behind in our payments, we will receive the following response, **"Pay your rent and then I will do something about it!"** No amount of pleading, excuses, or sad stories will change his mind.

So it is with us. Your body is the house you live in. You did not build it. God did. Your tithes are the rental fee you pay to your heavenly Landlord while you live here on earth. He has commissioned His ministers to collect His rent monies, i.e., our tithes.

When something goes wrong with our 'plumbing,' we lodge our complaint with Him. If we have been faithful in bringing our tithes to His storehouse, He is obligated to fix the problem or damage. If we have been withholding our tithes and/or sending them to our favorite evangelist, Bible teacher, pastor, missionary, etc., He is under no obligation to fix the problem.

Some people split their tithes. They send a little here, a little there, and a little for the local church. God says, *"Bring ye ALL the tithes into the storehouse."* (Emphasis mine.) **ALL THE TITHES – THE WHOLE TITHE – NOT A PORTION OF THE TITHES.**

Many years ago I heard Oral Roberts say, "If you can contain your blessings, you have never proved Malachi 3:10." This is the only verse in the Bible where God says, *"Prove me now herewith saith the LORD of hosts, if I will not open you the windows of heaven, and pour you out a blessing, that THERE SHALL NOT BE ROOM ENOUGH TO RECEIVE IT."* (Emphasis mine.) God is asking us to put him to the test NOW. Not tomorrow, but NOW.

The Second & Third Tithes

That there is a second and third tithe is shocking news for some but joyful news for others who have a spirit of giving.

Many years ago, an Orthodox Rabbi told me that every observant Jew gives thirty percent of his income to God, i.e., he gives three tenths of his earnings to the Lord.

The Second Tithe is the tithe on our increase from year to year. *"Thou shalt truly tithe on all the increase of thy seed, that the field bringeth forth year by year."* Deuteronomy 14:22

How do you do this? Each year you compare your gross earnings with the gross earnings of the previous year. If there has been an increase, you tithe on that increase. For example, this year you made $500 more than you did the previous year. Your tithe on the increase is $50.

You bring that tithe to the House of the Lord and mark it on your envelope, **'Second Tithe, tithe on my increase.'**

The third tithe is found in Deuteronomy 14:28, ***"At the end of three years thou shalt bring forth all the tithe of thine increase the same year."***

How is this third tithe made up? You compare your gross earnings of the third year with your gross earnings of the first year, and you tithe on that increase as well as the yearly increase which is your Second Title. Let us suppose that the difference between the amounts of the first and third year if $750, your third tithe would be $75. You bring that amount with you to the House of the Lord and mark it on your envelope.

"Tithe of the Third Year Increase."

The third year tithe is to be used for the assistance of the Levite, the stranger within our gates, the fatherless and the widow. (Deut. 14:29)) The local ministry is to ensure that the third tithe is used for this purpose and this purpose only.

Appendix II: The Lord's Portion - Tithes and Offerings

First Fruits And Offerings

What are First Fruit Offerings? We read previously that we are to honor the Lord with the first fruits of our increase. This is simply bringing the first portion of our annual pay increase as a **'First Fruit Offering'** to the House of the Lord and mark it so on the offering envelope.

There are a variety of other offerings in the Scriptures. There are **Thank Offerings.** Every time God answers a prayer, bring a **Thank Offering** to the House of the Lord and mark it so on your envelope. When the Lord heals you, bring a **Thank Offering** to the House of the Lord.

There are **Peace Offerings, Vows, Building Offerings, Alms, Food Offerings, Missionary Offerings,** as well as giving to **The Necessity of the Saints.** There are many more besides these. As you read your Bible you will come across others. It has been said that on the average, one in every five texts in the Bible refers to giving.

God says, *"The liberal soul shall be made fat: and he that watereth shall be watered also himself."* Proverbs 11:25

A. Ronald Coady

APPENDIX III

A Definition of Wisdom

What does the Bible mean by the word, 'wisdom'? The following quotation from Eugene H. Peterson's introduction to his paraphrase of the Book of Proverbs is the clearest definition I have read. I quote in part.

"In our scriptures, heaven is not the primary concern, to which earth is a tag-along afterthought. 'On earth *as* it is in heaven' is Jesus' prayer.

"'Wisdom' is the biblical term for this on-earth-as-it-is-in-heaven everyday living. Wisdom is the art of living skillfully in whatever actual conditions we find ourselves. It has virtually nothing to do with information as such, with knowledge as such. A college degree is no certification of wisdom – nor is it primarily concerned with keeping us out of moral mud puddles, although it does have profound moral effect up on.

"Wisdom has to do with becoming skillful in honoring our parents and raising our children, handling our money and conducting our sexual lives, going to work and exercising leadership, using words well and treating friends kindly, eating and drinking healthily, cultivating emotions within ourselves and attitudes toward others that make for peace. Threaded through all these items is the insistence that the way we think of and respond to God is the most practical thing we do. In matters of everyday practicality, nothing, absolutely nothing, takes precedence over God."*

James the Apostle writes:

"If any of you lack wisdom, let him ask of God, that giveth to all men liberally and upbraideth not: and it shall be given him." James 1:5

*Quotation taken from *THE MESSAGE.* Copyright 'Eugene H. Peterson, 1993, 1994, 1995. Used by permission of Nav Press Publishing Group.'

APPENDIX IV

Securing Gainful Means Of Employment

If you are going to build a personal fortune, you will need to be engaged in gainful employment.

Everyone enjoys doing the kind of work for which he is best suited. America offers a complete range of occupations that will meet everyone's needs.

First, you must decide **exactly** the kind of job you want. If it doesn't already exist, perhaps you can create it. (I hope I have not offended anyone's religious sensitivity.)

Second, choose the company or the person for whom you wish to work.

Third, study your prospective employer, policies, personnel and opportunities for advancement.

Fourth, analyze yourself, your gifts and talents, your capabilities and decide **what it is that you have to offer** to this company.

Fifth, get rid of the Oliver Twist mentality, **"Please Sir, may I have some more?"** He said this holding his small porridge bowl up to the orphanage manager. You are not going out with the attitude, **"Please Sir, do you have a job for me?"**

When you left school or college, you were encouraged to assembly a one page resume. In my years of experience, I have found that a one page resume is useless and hardly ever does what it is supposed to do: obtain gainful employment for you. I want you to forget all that you have been taught on preparing that one page resume and move into the realm of creativity.

The first thing you need to do is prepare a **written profile** on yourself. It will be called your **PERSONAL PROFILE.** Remember, in preparing your profile you aim to **inform, instruct, delight and persuade.** It should be typewritten, contain all pertinent information, bound in a suitable binder, and follow exactly the following format, changing it and improving it only as your creative imagination suggests.

1. **The Title page**
2. **Index**

Appendix IV: Securing Gainful Means Of Employment

3. Personal Data & Vital Statistics
4. Education
5. Ongoing Education
6. Specialized Training
7. Work Experience
8. References & Referees

The title page should look like this:

Personal Profile & Qualifications

Of

(Your first name, middle initial, and last name)

Applying for the Position of

(Name of the position)

with

(Name and address of the Company)

It should be framed within a border.

Page 1 should read as follows:

The Personal Profile of
(Your name as it appears on the Title Page)

Table of Contents

<u>Page #</u>
1. Personal Data & Vital Statistics………………..
2. Education……………………………………….
3. Ongoing Education…………………………….
4. Specialized Training……………………………
5. Work Experience……………………………..
6. References and Referees………………………..

Your Copyright notice will appear at the bottom of this page. It will read as follows:

©Copyright (year): This Personal Profile is copyright, and may not be copied, Photostatted or duplicated, either in total or in part, without the prior written permission of (your name.)"

Appendix IV: Securing Gainful Means Of Employment

The Personal Profile of (your name)
On the opposite side there will be pasted a recent wallet sized photo of you. (Have this taken at a professional studio.)

Personal Data
<u>Vital Statistics</u>

Place of Birth:
Date of Birth:
Citizenship:
Countries Lived In: (if applicable)
Life's Partner: (First name of spouse)
Married: (Date and place of marriage)
Children: (Names of children)
Grandchildren: (If applicable)
Hobbies: (List your hobbies)
Sports Activities: (List present and past sports engaged in)

Further state if you are a non-alcoholic drinker, non-smoker, and non-gambler. This is very important if your employer is considering you for a position of trust or handling large sums of cash.

Following this format, now prepare the other pages of your profile. When you have completed it, put all the pages in a clear plastic cover binder, and either hand carry it or mail it to the appropriate person at the Company where you desire to be employed.

I assure you will at least get an interview. If there is not a position available for you, they may create one to fit your aptitude.

Remember, you are not going out looking for a job. Rather, you are marketing your services. Someone out there is looking for someone like you and wants to hire your talents.

When you go to a studio to have your photograph taken, PLEASE dress in suit, collar and tie. When you go for your interview, depending on the position you are seeking, dress appropriately.

Offer to go to work on a **trial basis.** This may appear radical, but it seldom fails to win at least a trial. If you are sure of your qualifications, then a trial is all you need. Such an offer demonstrates your confidence in your ability to fill the position you seek. It also demonstrates your determination to have the job and the conviction of your prospective employer's decision to hire you permanently after the trial period.

Remember, you are marketing your services.

Epilogue

My task is done. I have provided you with your Seven Building Blocks and all the necessary materials you need in building your house of 'personal fortune." It is not up to you to apply the principles set forth in this book. You stand on the verge of success. My prayers are with you. I know that the Lord will guide you and bless you as you build your house.

In closing, I remind you of the words of Jesus:

"Therefore, whosoever heareth these sayings of mine, and doeth them, I will liken him to a wise man, which built his house upon a rock: And the rain descended, and the winds blew, and beat upon that house; and it fell not: for it was founded upon a rock." Matthew 7:24-25

In this book you have **'rock-solid'** teachings and wisdom. Don't delay. Commence building today, and say with Nehemiah of old:

"The God of heaven, he will prosper us; therefore we his servants will arise and build." Nehemiah 2:20

Personalize it and affirm with a loud voice: ***"The God of heaven, he will prosper me; therefore I his servant will arise and build."***

Do not waste valuable time in defending your position and explaining what you are doing. Speak to your opposition and say with Nehemiah,

"I am doing a great work, so that I cannot come down; why should the work cease, whilst I leave it, and come down to you?" Nehemiah 6:3

About The Author

Ron Coady is a retired bishop of the Orthodox Church of the British Isles.

He was born in Sydney, Australia and came to an experiential knowledge of Jesus Christ as Lord and Saviour as a youth of seventeen years of age.

He met Muriel Fleming in 1946, and they were married on January 29, 1949. Two children were born of their union, Calvin and Joy.

On May 31, 1957, they migrated to New Zealand with Muriel's widowed mother, Florence Fleming. They settled in Tauranga in the North Island. Here their third child was born, Andrew, who died in infancy.

Ron served two years in the New Zealand armed forces. After being honorably discharged, he taught in the Tauranga Night Bible School. In 1959 he entered into his evangelistic and divine healing ministry. During this time he co-founded and founded twenty-five churches.

He published and edited a monthly magazine entitled *Revival News.* Within twelve months it reached a circulation of over ten thousand.

In 1967 he visited Davis, California, and started a church. In December 1968, he returned to Davis to pastor this church.

At the end of 1969 he returned to New Zealand and migrated with his family to the United States. They settled in Davis where he has resided ever since. He is a well-known Bible teacher and traveling evangelist.

Bishop Coady is available for speaking engagements and personal appearances. For more information contact the publisher at:

Bishop A. Ronald Coady
ADVANTAGE BOOKS™
PO Box 160847
Altamonte Springs, FL 32716

To order additional copies of this book or to see a complete list of all **ADVANTAGE BOOKS™** visit our online bookstore at:

www.advantagebookstore.com

or call our toll free order number at: 1-888-383-3110

Longwood, Florida, USA

"we bring dreams to life"™
www.advbooks.com

Printed in the United States
34976LVS00001B/169-279